# A Rosary of Poems
# Five Decades

## Jane Rades

Beatitude PRESS

BERKELEY, CALIFORNIA

ISBN:  978-0-9818859-3-3

# Contents:

*Dedication:*

Thank you to Sterling Bunnell, who gave me the idea to write poetry.

## The Lipstick Song
*(Fire and Ice)*

There never was fight
like the fight between
the fire and the ice.

The ice said to the fire
"I'll put you out good,
I'll be all cold and
freeze all your wood."

Said the fire to the ice,
"I'll melt you down,
I'll burn bright till
there's only water on this ground."

So they both kept their word,
and the ice melted fast,
and the fire was put out
by the water which flowed past.

## Shooting Stars

"The stars are out
and they might leave without us."
The moon might leave without us,
us on the earth, dallying and slow.

The stars might leave without us
and go to another solar system,
they're tired of us ruining their atmosphere.

They might leave without us,
leave us in a dark stage
on a shadowy earth.

We had taken them for granted
and they just took off.

## Today's Minestrone

Logos and Eros
logic and the imagination.
I think therefore
I do not create.

Balance the image and the thought
logic and the imagination
vice and versa
so justice is done
and I'm on both scales.

It's a logician's mess,
math doesn't refer to reality.
Tell that to an accountant
he'll try to convince you
the figures say one thing
and they just lie there
telling it all.

Math isn't real
it's somewhere between
the noodles left
in the bowl of soup
curlicues of alien reality.

## Death Equals Debt

I found out what death is, it is debt.
Financial skeleton in the closet.
Can't buy any new clothes.
The skeleton falls out of the closet,
just bare bones, that's all I can afford.

I think of debt as death
it's bones hanging from my neck
jewels of indulgence, polished perhaps
there for everyone to see.

Skull, pennies from heaven
on the sidewalk
and in store windows.
Crossbones, labels of warning.

Holes in a skull for eyes that see nothing,
golden teeth, shiny money.
Talk through a hole in your head,
and see if you can make cents.

## The American Way of Death

Turn in your grave, whirl in an urn,
scoff at ashes scattered
on certain beaches
and in many museums.

GRIND and pulverize to cornmeal consistency
so no bones show.
That's the American Way of Death.

## Through The Underworld

Through the underworld
underground, under world.

Foghorns in the distance
out in the ocean.
I'm crossing over the River Styx
been sliding all the way down it
sliding since I was six.

As the earth cracks
and the moon is eclipsed
as the earth quakes
and the end is sensed
I have faith in myself.

## A Travelogue

There were no condors in Peru,
nor orchids in Madagascar.
We saw tiny orchids on a mountainside,
and once in a garden.

But there were lemurs,
and if one could use the word "cute" to the 14th power,
I could describe the lemurs.

There was a sisal plantation,
so "ecological", so "green",
except rainforest had been cut down to plant it.
And, there were the rows of one room houses for the workers,
lined up,
green indeed.

And in Spain I saw a castle in ruins by the side of the road.
I thought it was a fake castle,
a bit of Disneyland,
but it *was* a ruined castle,
this was *Spain*.

There were spiders to eat in Cambodia
but I did not,
could not
indulge.

In Japan the seaweed moved on the plate,
waving to me.
Then I realized it was because it was paper thin.

And every country has its hat.
The only thing is how to get it back on the plane.

## Countries, What I Saw

*Cambodia*
The sight of a zebu, the national cattle
pulling a cart, carrying another zebu,
a butchered zebu.
Did it sense it?
I can still see it.
Symbol of a country
where one and a half million died
murdered by their own.

*Madagascar*
In the capital "Tana"
almost no street people
in this supposed "third world" country.
How do they do it?
And the children waiting silently
sitting a short distance away
waiting till we finished our lunch
waiting for the scraps.

*Mali*
The U.S.A.I.D. grain for sale
in the market in Timbuktu.
And letting a man, a "guide",
lead me across town to the library
of medieval books.
Something I wouldn't do in a million years
in this country.

*France*
Hell or high water,
I was going to get to the Costume Museum.
A 100,000 Frenchmen,
electrical workers striking.
I made my way
through the demonstrations,
and, the museum was closed
"for renovation".

*India*
In the Himalaya,
having our lunch on the mountainside.
A man and a young girl walking up,
her downcast look.
And the guide said
he's probably having sex with her
(his daughter)
She, no more than 10 years old,
but what could you do.

Or, a man walking into our campsite,
and asking the guide for medication
for his stomach.
Very sick, but what could you do,
out here, hundreds of miles
from doctors and hospitals.

*Spain*
At the hotel in Trujillo
the clerk pronounced my last name right,
and he pronounced Smith "smeedth".
It was the culminating moment
of international travel.

## Me a-boo abu

Abu – Simbel
Simba
Cimba Cimba
me the lion
temple of stone
moved so the dam
could overflow
and I would not drown
stone by stone
and reconstructed
miles away.
What did I mean?
What do I mean now?

a symbol
cymbal crashing
a big noise
that's what I am.
Not ancient,
un–occult
only animal
and bio–degradeable.
Abu, Abu
boo hoo boo
I cry
I crash
for my ancient
Egyptian masters.

## Egypt Remembered

Where is the connection again
between earliest memories
and how I think now?
I've lost the connection
between King Tut
and myself.

I'm afloat in an azure field,
with gold things sparkling all around,
and I can't see them,
reach out and touch them.

Ah yes,
I start to remember Egypt now.
I was Hatshepsut
or Nefertiti,
or both.

## Sunday Morning in New Mexico

Wet snow slip slops on the walls and gravel,
hints of California
and foggy soft rained days.

Snow melts as it hits the ground, never stays,
no icicles. Bare trees.
Earth loam mushes under the tires.

Breakfast tastes better on rainy off-days,
two cups of coffee, not one,
poem of a musical morning.

Ezra Pound in Italy, Mozart's last song,
the Sunday driver's pitch,
I rest in a station of hush.

Just tuning in to the key of outside,
no holy destinations,
muffler on the day's fuss button.

## Recollections in Young Adulthood

Festering ulcers,
the sharp glance to the side,
the halting smile,
the shy hi,
the stutter,
the daydream, the nightmare,
the uncertainty of life,
mortality rate of people under 25 years of age
the suicide rate in Sweden,
the hissing of the grain pouring down the chute
into the railroad car.

## Thoughts Upon Awakening

The socks
where do they disappear to
all of my black socks?
In the washer?
In the dryer?

Blackness of kitty
cat hair so soft
all over everything.
Omnipresent cat hair
and disappearing socks
are the sum total of my life to date.

## Traveling Back In Time

The map of our relationship
is up on the wall
you are always to one side
and I to the other.
Roads and playgrounds
and open space
free and windy,
overgrown with dry grass,
fennel, and remains of houses.

I call you from an empty lot
and we're both seven years old,
out of doors,
discovering old cars
abandoned in the woods
and wild raspberries.
I almost knew at the time
it was a wonderful
thing to remember.

## Having a Friend in the Hospital

I was thinking about this,
and it bumped the future up into the present,
that is, *now.*

*Now* is it,
no pork belly futures,
not a future in stocks and bonds
only green money,
not even a piggy bank.

Three little pigs all went home
all in a row.

Get your ducks in a row
your will
and your trust
and your advance healthcare directive.

The farmer is calling the cows home.
My Dad said they used to say
"cumbah cumbah"
and the cows came home,
like the saying,
"not till the cows come home".
Hearing my Mother say this
as if everyone understood
what it meant.

As it everyone understood
what the future held
in the palm of it's hand
outstretched and empty.

## The Invention of Clouds

I thought I'd invented clouds
but it turns out someone
had done it a long time ago.
Was he Greek?
Was he god?
Who is he anyway?

I'd known I was a god,
but not the same one,
a hot one,
but only in my head.

It's over my head
what's going on,
it's written in the clouds
what's happening.

## The Wedding

I was at a wedding
on an island
over a footbridge
on a small river,
a bright September day in the Midwest.
And the microphones faded in and out
but somehow it didn't matter.
People had gathered
to see the union.
They joked it had taken eleven years.

Crossing over to a union.
You better know what you're doing!
All of these people have traveled to see this!
There, as the river glittered by,
my aged parents
in plastic chairs on the riverbank,
unable to use the footbridge,
matriarchal and patriarchal,
a respect for age rarely seen.

Use the footbridge
to cross over.
It has a slight arch
and the wood is old.

Crossing over to the other side,
is it a mystery?
Is it like a footbridge
over a pretty river
a lovely walk over
to an island in the river
where a ceremony takes place
and people stand attentively
all dressed up
a union, an agreement,
a satisfaction.

And the water shines
and the river flows
and we float downstream
but it's not a dream.
We will wake up
and it will still be true.

## From Steve's Book
*(dedicated to my brother Stephen Rades – 1952-1992)*

In the hereafter
everybody came in from dead so black
you could never see it.

In death
everybody came in from white so light
you could never see it.

In the hereafter
everything is so blue
a bright, clear aquamarine
so clear you can drink out of it.

In the hereafter,
every day is sunny
so yellow you can drink it in.

Get some perspective!
Death so close,
in clouds so full of rain they could burst
so far away
in a sky so gray
it doesn't matter.

*Remember the good things.*

## My Friend Johnny
### *(Through The Looking Glass)*

Roads intersect
lives intersect
people double back
or come in again
and you get a nibble.

Then you think
oh, this could turn
into a real friendship,
and then they are dead.

## Remembering Mother Goose

One sunny morning, quiet in my kitchen,
       eating my harmony grits,
I chanced to see a book, thrown in the corner,
       with the sun shining on it.
I put down my spoon, went over to look,
       and saw it was my old Mother Goose
that I'd read as a child, unchained in a world
       I knew when I was loose.

The book in my hand, I went back to my chair
       and opened it's golden covers,
A tear came to my eye as I read these rhymes
       of all my friends and lovers.
I picked up my spoon and the book talked to me
       in a voice that echoed clear.
And I listened, quite sane, afraid for my ears,
       of what I might or might not hear.

*It said, "awake, arise put out your eyes*
       *and hear what time of day*
*and when you have done, pull out your tongue*
       *and see what you can say.*
*If wishes were horses beggars would ride*
       *and the lovers would be side by side,*
*but all our turns come around, we're lost and we're found,*
       *you'll get yours and I'll get mine."*

I used to live in the country near London town,
       I saw the bridges come falling down,
and the Highwayman came riding and I saw him at night
       and he rode away before it got light.
I went with old Mother Hubbard to check her cupboard,
       and I too saw it was bare.
And I knew the Old Woman who lived in a shoe
       and neither did I know what to do.

And I went with Little Bo Peep, who'd lost her sheep,
     and I said, "please stop your cryin,
there's all kinds of things happening out there while you weep,
     all kinds a people are dying".
She said, "Oh, sometimes I'm bad, I rave and complain,
     I accuse and arrest and I don't talk plain.
And when I'm hungry they throw me a bone,
     and when nobody's with me I'm always alone."

But then she said, reassuring, that any wish told,
     is sure to come true be it ever so old.
And I smiled as I left, hoping she's right,
     resolving to tell all my wishes that night.
Sunny morning, back in my kitchen,
     finished with my harmony grits,
I rose from my table, closing the book,
     and took it to where the sunlight could shine on it.

*With a flash it came then, all it had been,*
     *and I wanted to say thank you,*
*to the people within these pages so thin,*
     *for being my friends as I grew.*
*And it they were real, like they had been,*
     *I think they'd have thanked me too.*

## Me and The World

It all boils down to oil and gas
how much there is
how much is left
if there is any.

Whole countries boiled down
peoples subjugated
so we can drive our cars
pedal to the metal.

Whole bodies discarded
the worst faux pas
un-imaginable.

The world took a turn
for the better this week.
This week was a nightmare for me.
Maybe it follows
that as long as I'm behaving badly
the world will be OK.

Hard to tell.

## Joseph Cornell, Artist
*(after seeing the exhibition at SFMOMA)*

Cabinets of curiosities,
a Victorian idea.
I love Cornell's boxes.
I feel like I'm *in* them,
the girl at the window,
Hedy Lamar in the bluish interiors and misty landscapes.

I'm trying to get in touch with them,
but it's an elusive reality,
someone *else's* dreams,
interiors untouched,
facades unbroken,
glacial extremes in the southern hemisphere.

Will global warming melt all the ice?
We think so now.
I just worry about the polar bears,
great white clumps of fur.
And their cubs, the baby bears.
What are *they* doing?
Can they swim in the warm water?
Will they adapt?
I reach out to touch them, but they are wild things,
as in wild dreams,
I have no right.

Admire from afar, like Cornell's boxes,
right there,
but they might as well be a million miles away,
a million light years away.

Like the stars,
the baby bears,
like the stars
my dreams.

I live in a cold wasteland of ice,
too cold to touch.

## The Piano Lesson

Blackfriars, blackbirds
black coats flutter
did I see them
or see a shadow
or only imagine.

My father dropped
me off early in the morning
before school
to take a piano lesson
in the back of the convent.

Six floors lined with porches
an occasional elderly nun
small, walking slowly
long black habit ruffling
layers of black cloth swaying.

Up a staircase
old, dark varnished stairs
creaking with each step
to a plain room
with a piano in it
and not much else.

Blackness and whiteness of keys
little mirrors into this past
tiny windows, vignettes,
memory only makes it hazier.
It seemed so clear for so long
and now I'm not sure
how it really was
and I never did learn
to play the piano.

A long way from this,
living alone in an apartment,
listening to the buses outside
going off their trolleys
hearing the traffic in the rain
the neighbors playing
one Linda Ronstadt tape all night.

And not an artist
after all that.
All the thought that had gone into it,
all the work that was put into it.
Life's meaning,
raison d'être,
being cut off,
and I am cast off.

## Objects

Objects of the past
make me remember the present,
remembrance of things in the interim,
the present is present
in these objects I have collected on my trips,
from my traveling.

Transformation of objects,
but they aren't supposed to mean anything.
I'm supposed to be spiritual,
the material shouldn't matter.

Yet I see worlds
in this little wooden motorcycle
from Madagascar, bought for $1.50.
Moving parts with different colors of woods and polished.
Bought at a roadside stand,
a house by itself at the side of the road,
children selling,
for what I pay for a cup of coffee here.

Looking at the object I see the house
and wonder about the children.
The object is enveloped in feelings,
wooden and warm,
radiating from a world within.

## Disguised As A Bag Lady

I stare at the bag lady
across the street.
She was there yesterday morning too,
on the corner
looking at the traffic.
For some reason
she picks up her bags
and walks up Vallejo Street.

Where does she go?

I was headed in her direction.
I could have been a bag lady.
Maybe I am one,
I'm just better dressed.
My friend said,
you'd never know how I felt
by the look of my clothes.
I didn't give away anything,
not even in a plain brown wrapper.

**Louis's Glass Factory**     *(Louis Tiffany)*

Full blown flower vases
I cannot imagine the color of.
Tiffany glasses
layers of lenses
shards in the desert one day
a cathedral window the next.

**Louise's Glass Factory**     *(Louise is my middle name)*

We moved out to Elm Grove
and I started kindergarten,
painting for the first time,
stroking the paint on the paper,
a flat, stubbed brush,
dressed in a bright blue smock
with tiny yellow flowers on it.

Mother made curtains
for our bedroom,
white sheets with crayoned-on
circus animals.

The first sunny summer
and there was space
like I'd never dreamed.
Hunting for arrowheads,
golf balls, butterflies, thorn apples.
Inner Sanctum broadcasting,
laying on the rug in our bathrobes,
as close as we could get to the radio.

Maybe I had a happy childhood
and am just now realizing it.
Then again,
maybe I'm looking at it through
Tiffany glasses, layers of lenses,
shards in the dust one day
a cathedral window the next.

## Peeling the Onion

Peeling away the layers
of craziness
is like peeling an onion
and it makes my eyes cry too.
I think I have gotten down to it
and then another layer is revealed.

Wear garlic
it's good for you.
Put it in the soup of life
along with the onions,
striped of the parchment skin,
sweet and strong,
edible.

## In a Parallel Universe, or My Life In a Nutshell

I'm a schizophrenic, *in extreme remission*,
so I exist in a parallel universe.
Kind of like a bike lane
running alongside the highway,
chattering away to myself,
all of my rants,
knowing none of it is true.

Every once in a while it spills out,
like splashing inky wine
all over clean sheets.
People aghast or embarrassed,
no way to really repair the damage.

But then again,
I'm not in an institution,
a green-walled, metal bed *facility*.
I live a *normal* life,
very boring
and some would say dull.
In fact, I probably appear to do nothing.

When I first got out of the hospital
it was enough just to have survived.
I started to do better
and bought some nice clothes.
But after a couple of years
that feeling faded.

I used to wish I could trade it in,
(the paranoia,)
for one of the other ones,
like manic-depression, or bi-polar
as it seems like the meds for those
really knock it out.

Now, I'm lucky just to be holding down a job,
as long as I stay organized I'm OK.
And, none of my friends know,
I've never told any of them.

## I Sent Messages

I sent messages did you hear them?
off into blue space,
from a dark place.
I sent messages did you get them?

Ideas born in a rain space,
ideas born in a blue place,
I'm in a dark place,
a black space,
I'm a shadow,
Did you get them?

She dreams that's what she does.
She sent you messages
from a blue space
in a rain space
rain, rain go away.
She sent you messages,
did you hear them?

Oh, I was just dreaming again,
about how it might have been
or how I thought it was.
She dreams,
that's what she does.

## Glass Castle for A Brain

I faced them and I felt like my face was glass,
that they could see everything I think.
I hadn't realized that this is another facet of paranoia.

Make it like glass blocks,
opaque and solid,
so no one can see in.

Glass castles, sand castles,
the hourglass runs out.
An hourglass of a figure,
standing in my own sand.

Glass shattering, and it glitters in the sand.
I cannot pick the pieces out,
be careful not to step on them!

*Poor feet*, exposed to everything,
not quite like walking on hot coals,
but it's not magic.

The glass becomes stained glass,
and I'm in the church of myself.

## After Thirty Years of Therapy

Correlation does not equal causality,
he's said it again and again.

My mind is like a bombed out World War II building,
the first tier filled with rusted iron girders,
rafters and walls scattered everywhere.

The second tier is netting and ropes,
twisted and torn.

The top tier is spider webs,
fragile and iridescent,
impossible to pick apart and resting on each other.

Everything is interwoven.
Try to construct *reality* from this!

If only there was something stronger,
like walls and ceilings,
barriers and stairs,
to go from one area of consciousness to another.
If only there was a way to experience clarity!

I need organization!
my mind is a dustbin of history and emotions,
dubious conclusions,
doubtful memories.
Somebody swept up the floor and dumped it all here.
Find that cleaning lady!

I never know what to do,
I'm not sure what has happened.
I just kind of plod on
to a future that is sure to be fertile
and filled with light.

## Description of a Drawing

Unwittingly I drew Rembrandt and had him first labeled as the cook (kook) responsible, a French chef, I thought. But then I remembered waking up and seeing the empty canvas stored in the rafters above my bed filled with a smiling full-color self portrait of Rembrandt.

The "kook" was Rembrandt, the dutch lady was by his side, so I drew a lizard monster crawling from behind his hair and left the chef's hat on him. The lady has a butcher knife stuck in her head and she is mumbling to the side "Delacroix".

## After a Painting by Giovanni di Paolo

Paradise was when
they all wore long gowns
and headdresses and lots
of beads and walked
around the court
and some got beheaded
and some ate grapes
in the arbors
and sat in sculptured gardens,
frail and smelling
(they didn't have deodorants).

Very short lives
but it looks like
paradise from here.

## Don't Let That Kitty Out

Don't let that kitty out
it's raining out and cold.
Don't let the kitty out
it's wet out and she'll die.
She'll catch cold and die
don't let her out.
She'll get her feet wet
and they're hard to dry out.

She wants to catch birds
and hop over fences,
but it's raining outside,
don't let her out the door.
Today she's staying inside,
shove her back with your foot.
No out today,
no play out.
Far off tomorrow is the day
she can go way out.

Now she sits by the window
and licks herself down,
kitty wants to go out,
don't let her out,
today, kitty's rain-bound.

## The Petsitting Chronicles

First of all, I should have been able to interview the cats,
not the owners,
and I would have found that the missus was an alcoholic
or completely nuts.

Finding myself newly unemployed,
there I was,
living in a condo on Union Street,
with a car to drive.
It astounded me
what people would do for their cats.

I started petsitting
because I was in debt.
I gave up my apartment,
got an answering service and a P.O. box.

Sometimes floundering,
with no place to live the *very* next day,
I always scraped through.
An afternoon or two spent in my car,
parked down at the Marina Green.
All of my possessions in the back seat of the station wagon,
I ate and read the paper.

I learned that a place itself could not make people happy.
It didn't matter how beautiful the building
or how great the neighborhood.
*Misery was misery, no matter where it lived.*

Nomadic existence,
living nowhere, but everywhere.
Impermanence.
Maybe I was finally living in the French way,
existentially,
or maybe I was a Buddhist,
and just didn't know it.

## All Birdie, All the Time
### (about my four year old cat, Birdie)

I call him my little sweetie,
what a smarty,
what a cutie,
but he just bit me for the third time.
I swabbed it with alcohol.
Last June it was $125 for a doctor's visit,
and an antibiotic for a cat bite.
My sweetheart,
the alpha cat in the house,
so pretty with his long black and grey hair.

I got him from the vet at six months
he had fallen out of a window
so he only has three legs.
I got a cut rate, $75 instead of $100.

He almost got returned to the vet,
as he chewed up two sets of venetian blinds,
and shredded the mail a couple of times.

If I got him trimmed
it would make his grooming easier,
but would it make him a happier cat?
I think maybe I'm too nice to him,
it's a good thing I never had kids.

But now I have resigned myself,
that some days he is just a very busy kitty.


*Postscript: On July 3, 2008 Birdie bit me while I was brushing him.
Two days later I was in the ER, IV antibiotic, x-rays, wrist cast.
Cost, $1,179.00.*

**Gardenia**

Sun action shown yet
in dead twisted leaves of wood green.
A crisp brown thing that was once Gardenia.
A lemon yellow shooting star of fragrance
hanging in the air.


**Rain Painting**
*(description of a Navaho sand painting)*

Raingirl carries rain rope and sun ray,
feathered rainbow flying over.
Over Rainboy,
feathered protecting black and white lightning.

While traveling on rainbow arcs
the female proceeds with the male
in a sunwise direction.

Circular rainbow bars around a central lake,
dragonflies and moisture clouds,
grey smudges,
sealing.

**Droning**

The light reflects off the wings
of the flies on the outdoor patio.
They are pretty (the flies).

The light shimmers on the leaves
at a nice angle.
The spider webs are illuminated
in the sun.

The drone of small conversations,
I can't hear them,
my ears must be bugged.

## Those Blooming Orchids

The orchids bloom in the house
delicate pinkish-lavender,
they last for weeks,
then wilt.

In their wild state
they bloom from the trees.
In *our* wild state
we lived in tree houses
and looked at the orchids
and only came down
to look for food.

We had parrots for pets
and we were mostly
vegetarian.

Then, we were orchids,
now, we are simply late bloomers.

## To The Jaguar

Last night I saw you in the dark,
when I walked past you winked.
Take care of yourself, be smart,
so you won't become extinct.

Palm trees flutter lightly as you go in search of game,
to me your life seems nicer, it's not easy being tame,
you are an animal, you're free and you're strange.

Today I saw you out, lonely and afraid,
you roared at the wind and blew it far away,
don't let yourself die out, be careful where you lay.

It's true I'm of the race of man,
born free but everywhere in chains,
but I look into your jaguar eyes,
you go away, the fire remains.
You are an animal, you need a place to stay.

Sleeping in a jungle tree I hear you softly purr,
you move a lot leaving just a trace of where you were,
don't let the hunter get you for your pretty fur.

Last night I saw you in the dark,
when I walked past you winked.
Take care of yourself, be smart,
so you won't become extinct.

## At The Beach

I saw two seagulls today
down on the sand
near the waves washing in.
They were talking to each other,
beeping back and forth,
their necks going from side to side
in a kind of rhythm,
one answering the other,
asking "where are the kids?"
or "have you found anything to eat yet?"
and things like that,
whatever seagulls say to each other.

## Circle In the Sand

Make an offering to the lord, greet the star in the north
make a circle in the sand, in the center make a stand.
In the cool morning air, draw with a stick in your hand,
make an offering to the sky, that you might fully understand.

The sun is just a ball of gas, a million years the earth should last.
So make a stand upon the land, pray not to god but to man.

Make an offering to a cloud, that natural rain will fall,
say it loud, so the cloud will hear your call.
And then you'll know what to do, as sure as oceans are blue
and what you do will be good, as sure as forests are wood.

In the cool morning air, walking on the sand
make an offering to the sky that you might fully understand,
offer to the dawning sun, as it rises in its place,
see the circle round the sun and see it face to face.

Offer to the east that grass will grow for gentle beasts.
Offer to the west that birds will still come home to nest.
Offer to the north that kings and queens will still go forth.
Offer to the south that in this kingdom man is not cast out.

And being careful to hear what they might say, listening to their side,
you'll know more and more how you can save the land and tide.
And as it's quiet and the waves roll in you might hear the earth as she
cries out to you in the wind, she cries, "oh save what's left of me".

Little drops of blue make the ocean move in harmony,
little grains of sand make the land roll in melody
and it's all in the right key, nothing out of tune,
all in the right key except for the human.

## Fountain Pen

A fountain of words
treading water
walking all over the words
that's what poetry is.

## *About the Author:*

Jane Rades was born in Wisconsin in 1942. She moved to San Francisco in 1963 and has lived there ever since except for a year in Santa Fe, New Mexico. She has traveled to Mali, Madagascar, Peru, India, France, Germany, Austria, England, Turkey, Cambodia, Mexico and Spain. She attended the University of Wisconsin-Milwaukee and received a B.A. in Painting from the San Francisco Art Institute. In addition to writing she draws, paints and does photography.

She has read at local venues in San Francisco and Berkeley, including Bird & Beckett Books & Records, The Beat Museum, Café Prague, Sacred Grounds, Bibliohead Bookstore, Gallery Café, It's A Grind Coffee House, Poets In The Trees, and the Poets 11 Series for the Friends of the San Francisco Public Library.